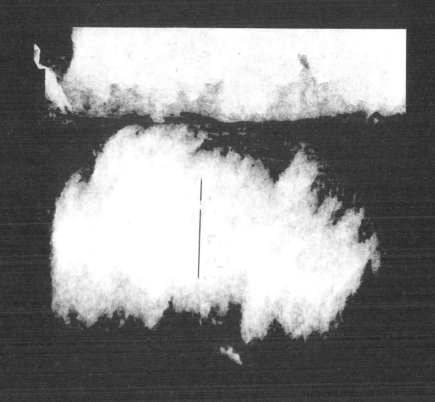

THE ALLEN
ILLUSTRATED GUIDE TO
HORSE
CLOTHING

THE ALLEN
ILLUSTRATED GUIDE TO
HORSE
CLOTHING

HILARY VERNON

J. A. ALLEN · LONDON

ISBN 0.85131.792.8

J.A. Allen
Clerkenwell House
Clerkenwell Green
London ECIR OHT

J. A. Allen is an imprint of Robert Hale Ltd

British Library Cataloguing in Publication Data
A catalogue record for this book is available from the British Library

Edited by Jane Lake
Design by Paul Saunders
Illustrated by Maggie Raynor

Printed in Hong Kong by Dah Hua International Printing Press Co. Ltd.

*I would like to dedicate this book to my mother Mrs June Vlies
who has always encouraged me in every venture, and from
whom I inherited my love of horses and animals.*

Contents

Acknowledgements

My thanks to Penny and Katie Jones for breaking and schooling all my youngsters while I am working and writing, to Quanah Holland, for allowing herself to be interviewed on the processes of rug cleaning and mending, and to Caroline Burt of J.A. Allen for her continued support.

1

The Principles of Rugging Horses

Reasons for Rugging-up

Several factors will help you decide whether you need to put rugs on your horse or pony.

The time of year

The horse will have a summer coat from the late spring until the weather begins to get colder in late September or early October. When this happens he will shed his summer coat and begin to grow a thick double coat to protect him against the impending cold weather. If your horse is to be stabled and worked during the winter period, then in order for him to be fit and healthy, and depending on the degree of work and level of fitness to be achieved, he will need to be clipped to some degree. When clipping a horse and depriving him of some of his thick protection against the cold, we have to substitute rugs for his own coat to keep him warm.

The type of horse or pony

A finely bred horse or a horse bred in a country without our range of weather simply will not grow enough winter coat to keep him warm in this country's harsh winter conditions. This type of horse will probably need to be rugged-up, even if not clipped, as the winter progresses.

It is most important that you know just how many and what type of rugs your horse or pony requires. You also need to make sure your horse is at the right temperature; we want to keep a horse warm but it is equally important that he is not continually uncomfortably hot with no way of alleviating the discomfort for himself. He should just feel warm under a rug particularly over the region of the back and loin area. If he feels very hot or sweaty then he is too hot. If, on the other hand, he feels chilled then obviously he needs extra warmth. You really need to work hard to keep your horse just comfortably warm particularly as there are such extremes of temperature in this country in the space of only a few days.

Human values

We have to be very careful not to impose human values and feelings on our horses. The majority of horses and ponies, particularly our own native breeds, were bred to live outside and, in the right conditions, thrive with very little interference from man. But, having said that, I am sure I am not the only one who has lain awake at night in severe weather and worried about my horses only to dash down in the morning to find them warm and cosy inside their rugs.

Differing environments

Horses have managed for centuries without turnout rugs so why do they need rugs now? The answer is that a lot of horses do not need rugs at all. If you can supply them with ideal conditions such as excellent grazing, ample differing types of shelter, well-drained spacious fields and plenty of fresh water then most horses will thrive with very little additional help but, if not, then you must use all means available to make sure your horses are comfortable and healthy and able to do the work you require of them which, without perfect conditions, is not always easy to do in the winter months. We can, however, make our horses' lives, and our own, more pleasant and easier by using the right sort and weight of turnout and stable rugs. If a horse does not need to utilise the food you feed him for warmth alone then it can also be channelled into maintaining general health and wellbeing.

Stabled horses' requirements also vary greatly. One stabled horse's needs may be very different from another's depending on the type and location of the stable. In a row of wooden boxes situated in a sheltered part of a yard, with wall insulation and wonderfully deep bedding, his particular rugging requirements are going to differ greatly from a horse say, in a stone box in an exposed part of the yard in the middle of a very severe winter in the north of England. You will find that these differing environments and individual horses will dictate how and what sort of rugs you use.

Feeding

The right sort of food plays a large role in keeping a horse warm, the saying 'an empty pony is a cold pony' is very true. A healthy horse or pony that has good quality hay ad lib and/or grazing and 24 hour access to clean water and adequate shelter is probably going to thrive in the winter months.

There is an art to feeding a horse or pony out in all weathers all winter. Your main aim is to keep him well fed with plenty of fibre and fresh water. During the day, horses will wander about quite happily foraging but as night falls and the temperature drops that is the time to make sure there is always plenty of hay and perhaps an additional feed if required. I do not think most people realise just how much hay should be consumed. When we advise people how to feed and what to feed, they will often say that they only give one or two slices of hay in the evening, which will realistically only last an hour or so, leaving the horse or pony with a possible 12 hours before any more hay is given. A medium-sized horse can consume half a bale of hay during the hours between 6 pm and until you see him the next morning. Unless your particular horse has a dietary problem he should always have enough hay safely available, particularly during the night, to keep him satisfied and to ensure he does not go hungry. If you have a horse who for some reason cannot have hay ad lib then a hay net given much later on at night will help to alleviate boredom and keep the gut active. Alternatively, the reduced hay ration could be fed in a horsehage net perhaps, so that it takes far longer for the hay to be consumed owing to the much smaller holes of this type of net.

A lot of digestive, stress and stable vices are caused by horses and ponies not having enough fibre in their diets and, therefore, if stabled, not enough to occupy them other than looking at four walls for hours on end.

Acquired Knowledge

We need to have the knowledge to know when to rug up and which rugs to use for different situations and horses. You must realise that just because someone on the yard where your horse is at livery has a certain rug, it will not necessarily follow that the same rug will fit your own horse or suit his own individual requirements. You have to take breeding and very different shapes of horses into consideration in particular, and what sort of clip, if any, your horse will have throughout the winter months.

Realistic Expectations

Do not forget to be realistic in your choice of rugs for your horse. If you have your horse at home or you do him entirely yourself then you can have as complicated a rugging system as you choose but in a livery yard situation it is best to simplify your horse's rugging needs. With the best will in the world it is unrealistic to expect a groom to rerug possibly 20 horses at a 10 pm late check, by removing all their rugs to put on an extra under-rug. It is far better to ask for a light top quilt to be placed over existing layers or possibly the outer rug removed to allow a thicker one to be put on instead.

2
Types of Horse and Their Rugging Requirements

The Old Horse or Pony

If you have a retired horse who is turned out all the time you may need to rug him just to protect him from the rain and wind as the winter progresses. Most healthy horses and ponies can cope well with cold dry conditions but when the weather is very wet and they are constantly wet and chilly, then they begin to feel cold and miserable and are not willing to move around to forage, which in turn makes them even colder as food means warmth.

As an old horse or pony will probably not be clipped he should not need a thickly padded rug. You should choose either a lightweight turnout rug that will ensure that he does not get too wet and will keep him dry and warm if it is wet and windy. If the weather begins to turn severe as the winter progresses, perhaps a turnout rug that is lightly quilted on the inside may be needed.

The Young Horse

The above information relevant to an old horse could also apply to a young horse as he will not be clipped or, probably, in much, if any, work. The most important thing to take in to consideration when rugging a young horse for the first time is to introduce new things carefully and gently and in a controlled environment. Always rug for the first time in a stable or small safe space from which he cannot escape. Once the rug is on, allow the youngster to get used to the feel of it for a period of time and allow him to move around with it on. Several of these sessions of being rugged and standing and moving around with a rug on in a stable should be practised before attempting to turn a young horse out for the first time in a rug. If your youngster is well handled then this should not be a problem but if he is not and shows signs of distress then it is best not to rug him up at all. I never turn young horses out in rugs that have leg straps, only in rugs with snug-fitting cross surcingles and a fillet string.

The Stabled Horse

How thick your turnout and stable rugs are will depend on whether your horse is clipped or not, what sort of clip your horse has, how long he will be out each day, what type of horse he is and how exposed the field is.

If your horse has a trace clip and is only out for an hour or so each day in a sheltered field, then a rug with a light or medium quilted lining will probably be sufficient, unless the weather turns very severe. If your horse is fully clipped and/or is out for long periods in the day and the weather is cold, then a heavier rug will be a necessity for both indoors and outdoors.

The Unclipped Horse

If you are not going to ride your horse, or only give him light work so that he is not going to sweat profusely, he will not, therefore, need to be clipped. Then, as long as the turnout conditions are reasonable, your horse will probably thrive without being rugged-up although that will mean that the colder it becomes the heavier his coat will be. The only real problem that will arise is that, when the horse is turned out again after exercise, he must be cool and dry which can be difficult with limited time if you are exercising at the end of the day when you have finished work. The thicker the coat the longer it will take for your horse or pony to dry out.

The Clipped Horse

A fully clipped, finely bred horse will need considerably warmer rugs than say a native pony with a trace clip: the finer the breeding and the more coat you clip off your horse the greater the rugging requirements become. As our climate is beginning to produce such variable temperatures it is probably better to work with a few layers of rugs rather than one enormously thick rug so that if the weather suddenly turns unexpectedly mild you can just remove a layer until the weather changes again.

The Horse Out at Grass All Winter

It is presumed that this category of horse is not very young or very old and is to be kept out all winter and not worked. If he has good grazing and, if necessary, a feed each day, he will probably not need a rug at all. If the winter is very severe or if it rains continuously, a lightweight rain rug could be used just to stop the horse being soaked by the rain every day and chilled by the wind.

3

Rug Sizes

RUGS ARE MEASURED in three-inch increments. Pony rugs usually range from 4 ft to 5 ft 6 in and horse-sized rugs from 5 ft 6 in to 7 ft 3 in. The rug is measured from the middle of the horse's chest around the point of the shoulder along the flank to an imaginary line drawn down from just in front of the top of the horse's tail.

Stable rugs do not have to cover the horse quite as efficiently from neck to tail as a turnout rug and do not have to allow for excessive movement and grazing. You may find that a stable rug can be a size smaller than a turnout rug. For instance, if your horse wears a 6 ft stable rug you may find that a 6 ft 3 in turnout rug fits well and gives more shoulder room and freedom to put the head down to graze.

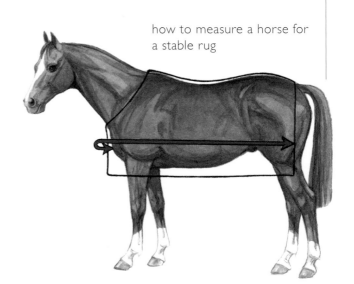

how to measure a horse for a stable rug

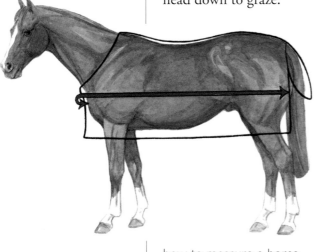

how to measure a horse for a turnout rug

Foals and very small and miniature ponies will need rugs specifically cut to fit their small stature.

Rug-size Chart

You may find that some horses require rugs that would not appear to be the right size for them. For example, a tall, long, lean horse may, in fact, require the same rug size as a shorter more cobby horse; the lean horse will take up the rug size in length and the cob will take up the rug size with the breadth of his chest. This chart gives you the approximate rug-size conversion measurements.

Approximate rug-size conversion chart

Horse's height in hands	Rug size in feet and inches	Rug size in centimetres
10.0	3 ft 3 in–3 ft 6 in	99 cm–107 cm
10.2	3 ft 6 in–3 ft 9 in	107 cm–114 cm
11.0	3 ft 9 in–4 ft	114 cm–122 cm
11.2	4 ft–4 ft 3 in	122 cm–130 cm
12.0	4 ft 3 in–4 ft 6 in	130 cm–137 cm
12.2	4 ft 6 in–4 ft 9 in	137 cm–148 cm
13.0	4 ft 9 in–5 ft	148 cm–152 cm
13.2	5 ft–5 ft 3 in	152 cm–160 cm
14.0	5 ft 3 in–5 ft 6 in	160 cm–168 cm
14.2	5 ft 6 in–5 ft 9 in	168 cm–175 cm
15.0	5 ft 9 in–6 ft	175 cm–183 cm
15.2	6 ft–6 ft 3 in	183 cm–190 cm
16.0	6 ft 3 in–6 ft 6 in	190 cm–198 cm
16.2	6 ft 6 in–6 ft 9 in	198 cm–205 cm
17.0	6 ft 9 in–7 ft	205 cm–213 cm
17.2	7 ft–7 ft 3 in	213 cm–221 cm

4

Outdoor and Turnout Rugs

Outdoor, turnout and New Zealand rugs all have the same job to do: they must fit well, keep out the cold, rain and wind and stay in place at all times whatever the horse or pony does without interfering with movement or compromising safety when he is turned out in the field, a yard or school. They come in a variety of different shapes, fastenings, outer materials and inner thicknesses.

If your horse is to be turned out all the time and not worked, it is very important that the turnout rug is checked regularly.

Regular Checks

You need to check twice each day that the rug is correctly in place and that there are no rubbed or sore areas. The rug should be removed at least twice a week and the horse given a light brush. Particular attention must be paid to the mane where the rug rests on it at the withers; each time you replace the rug you must run your hand under the neckline of the rug at the withers and lay the mane neatly the way it normally lies.

Rug rubs and pressure sores

Key areas that may get rubbed are: the hind legs, if the rug has leg straps, and the shoulder and chest areas where there is constant friction as the horse walks about and moves his head and neck up and down to graze. The withers are susceptible to pressure sores. The moment you see that the hair is being rubbed or the skin is bare, do something immediately before it becomes a major problem. If the shoulders are being rubbed, get a rug bib and treat the area with a cream to keep the skin soft, take away any inflammation and encourage hair regrowth. If the hind leg straps are chafing put some sheepskin or rubber tubing sleeves on them straight away. Treat the chafed areas with a soothing cream but do not try to harden the skin.

Types of Rug

Realistically most horses are going to need more than one rug, particularly if they are active working animals. Rugs are very expensive items so try to assess your own situation and work out how effectively and economically you can clothe your horse.

Lightweight rain rugs

This type of rug is very useful for autumn or at the beginning of the winter before it gets very cold and before you clip your horse, and equally as useful at the other end of the winter, moving into spring, when, as the weather improves, you do not need your horse to be so heavily clothed. It is simply a lightweight rug that has a thin waterproof outer shell with some sort of very lightweight lining, possibly a cotton, net or breathable nylon lining. It is designed to keep the wind and rain off the horse's back but, as it has no quilted inner, it will not make the horse too hot. This rug is also useful for keeping the wind and rain from chilling an older, less active horse as the winter gets more severe.

cross section of a lightweight rain rug

lightweight turnout rug

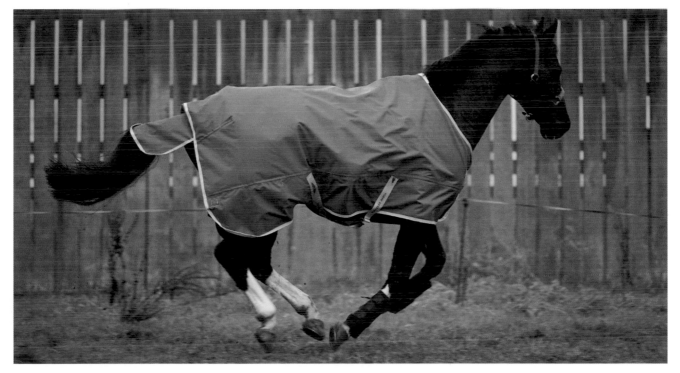

Middleweight turnout rugs

When the weather starts to get cold this rug will be very useful if you have clipped your horse with, say, a blanket clip. The outer should be completely waterproof and, in order to give a degree of warmth, it has some sort of lightweight quilting or wadding on the inside which is approximately 7 oz or 250 g. This rug is suitable for the middle winter months when the weather has begun to get colder but is not severe. It is an ideal turnout rug for an active horse who is turned out for a few hours each day and who would be too hot in a thicker rug. It is also useful for preventing a ridden pony in light work growing too large a coat and thus sweating profusely when worked.

cross section of
a middleweight
turnout rug

middleweight
turnout rug

Heavyweight turnout rugs

The outer is completely waterproof and has a very warm and thickly padded 12 oz or 14 oz (350 g or 400 g) quilt or inner wadding. It is suitable for a horse who has a full clip or a hunter clip and who is turned out during the day, or, perhaps, for Thoroughbred types who are turned out all the time in cold weather. This type of rug is extremely warm and can make horses very hot if they do not require that degree of warmth or if the weather turns unexpectedly mild.

cross section of a heavyweight turnout rug

heavyweight turnout rug

Turnout rugs with necks

Increasingly there are more and more turnout rugs being produced with neck-pieces attached to, and incorporated in, the neckline of the rug. Recently, the design of this type of rug has improved dramatically so that now the fit is very good and the fastenings much stronger. You are able to get every weight of rug from lightweight rain to heavyweight turnout with an attached neckpiece. There is no doubt that these rugs save a lot of grooming time because far more of the horse is covered up. And when time is precious in a busy working week, less time spent scraping mud off your horse means more time to exercise. The only real drawback is that there is constant friction on the mane area and can mean rubbed areas if your horse already has a thin mane and is to wear this type of turnout rug for hours on end.

turnout rug with a neck

New Zealand rugs

New Zealands are made of waxed cotton or canvas. These rugs are deep cut, i.e. as you look at the rug on a horse from the side, the rug sides should cover the horse almost to the knee at the front and the hock at the back. They usually have two straps at the chest and leg straps at the back and sometimes at the front as well. They are self-righting which means that if the horse gets down to roll, however enthusiastically, the rug always settles back into place as he gets up again.

Canvas turnout rugs

There are still many types of canvas turnout rugs on the market, some are very well cut and lined, some are not. The traditional canvas rug should be made of good quality dense pliable canvas lined with an equally good quality wool blanket. They normally come in two main styles: self-righting rugs usually have two breast straps and are deep cut with crossed hind leg straps, or they can be fastened with cross surcingles at the belly and two breast straps. The most important things to look for in a traditional canvas rug is that it is well cut and lined at the shoulders and that the neck hole is not too large. If the neck is too large the rug will pull back and lie behind the horse's withers and hang down too low on the shoulder thus causing rubbing.

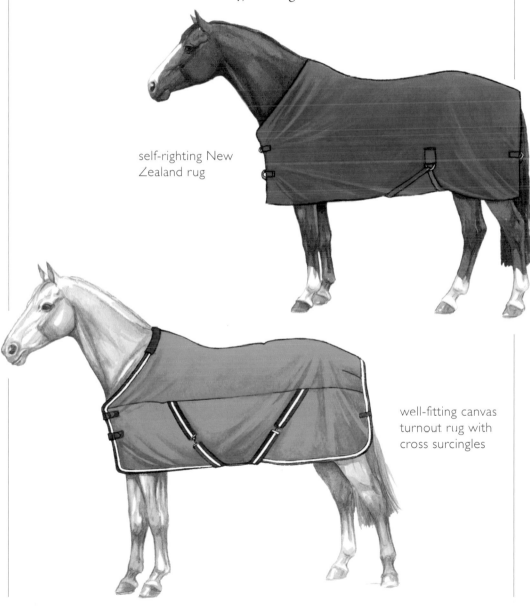

self-righting New Zealand rug

well-fitting canvas turnout rug with cross surcingles

Buying a Turnout Rug

When you buy a new rug, put it on in a clean dry environment and over a clean summer sheet. All good tack shops and equestrian outlets will change rugs for a different size or type but the rug must come back as new so that it can be put back into shop stock.

TO FIT The fit of your horse's rug is very important. He needs room to move freely, to roll, to gallop, to buck and to graze without restriction or wear and tear on his skin, and without his rug slipping sideways or pulling back on his shoulders. If your horse is an in-between size then it is better to have the turnout rug just a little on the large size, particularly if it has a sewn-down tail flap. If the rug is too small it can rub the shoulders and if the tail flap is very tight the horse cannot raise his tail properly.

The neckline is crucial to the success of the fit of a rug in the shoulder region. A neckline that is too large for the horse will result in the rug gaping at the front at the shoulders and dropping down so that the neck edging rests on the points of the shoulders causing severe rubbing and the rug will pull back behind the withers causing pressure sores. If left, the shoulders and withers will be so sore that you will be unable to continue to rug the horse. Fasten the chest straps so that there is a hand's breadth between the front of the rug and the horse's chest.

The neckline should lie above the shoulders and approximately 2–4 in in front of the withers.

Cross surcingles should be fastened so that there is a hand's breadth between them and the horse's belly.

Leg straps should be linked through each other which will prevent them from rubbing the horse's inner thighs. They should be long enough to allow freedom of movement but not so long that the horse can catch his hind legs in them when he is rolling or lying down.

Rugs should cover the horse from just in front of the withers to the tail and should be deep enough to hang below the belly line. *See* the photo on page 23.

5

Indoor, or Stable, Rugs

OBVIOUSLY THERE cannot be any hard and fast rules for how many rugs or what degrees of warmth an individual horse will need and, as stated before, there are many factors – the weather, stabling, clip and type of horse or pony – that contribute to an individual's requirements. This chapter details the rug types and weights available so that the right combination can be chosen for your horse or pony and differing situations.

I have read dozens of rug catalogues that all seem to differ slightly in their rug-fill weight conversions, so the chart below gives approximate rug-fill conversion figures.

Approximate rug-fill weight conversion chart

Ounces	Grams
4 oz	150 g
6 oz	200 g
8 oz	250 g
12 oz	350 g
14 oz	400 g
16 oz	450 g

Remember that the warmth of the rug also depends on the density of the outer layer of the rug.

Quilted Rug Weights

4 oz or 150 g
This lightweight quilted rug is suitable for just keeping the chill off. It should be used as the first rug when you begin to start rugging-up in the autumn and

also as the last rug used in the spring as the weather is beginning to get warmer and the horse is nearly ready to go without rugs. At these times of year, depending on the weather of course, you may be just rugging-up at night. This type of rug is very useful as an extra layer if the weather really begins to get cold and is also useful for unclipped older animals and youngsters who would benefit from a little extra warmth in the stable at night.

cross section of a 4 oz quilted rug

6 oz or 200 g

This rug is another lightweight rug which is also useful in the winter when two 6 oz rugs can be put on your horse at night to give him the warmth of a 12 oz rug.

8 oz or 250 g

This rug is suitable for rugging your horse up at night as the weather begins to get colder if, perhaps, you are using a 4 oz rug in the day. Then, as the weather changes, you could use the 8 oz rug during the day and both the 4 oz and the 8 oz at night making the total thickness of the night rugs 12 oz.

cross section of an 8 oz quilted rug

12 oz or 350 g

A much heavier and warmer rug, this is suitable for a horse who is clipped out. As the weather gets colder, it could be used during the day and then used in conjunction with an under-rug, or a 4 oz rug, at night. Alternatively you could use an 8 oz rug during the day and the 12 oz rug at night for a horse who is not fully clipped.

cross section of a 12 oz quilted rug

14 oz or 400 g

This very warm and substantial stable rug is suitable for a fully clipped-out horse in the middle of winter. This weight of rug is extremely warm and probably will not need any extra rugs used with it. You could use a 12 oz rug during the day and this rug at night, depending on the stabling and type of horse.

section of a 14 oz quilted rug

16 oz or 450 g

Not all manufacturers supply 16 oz rugs in this country and, as our winters are mild, they are not usually necessary.

Types of Rug

Jute rugs

At one time every horse had a jute rug, which was secured by a roller or a sewn-on surcingle, either unlined or lined with wool rugging. As the winter progressed you added layers of wool blankets underneath, folded and tucked under the roller on the outside of the rug at the withers. Today the quality of the jute does not seem as pliable and as dense as it used to be and the biggest drawback is that the rugs are not as easy to maintain as the lighter weight nylon stable rugs which are easy to sponge off and much easier to wash than the traditional jute.

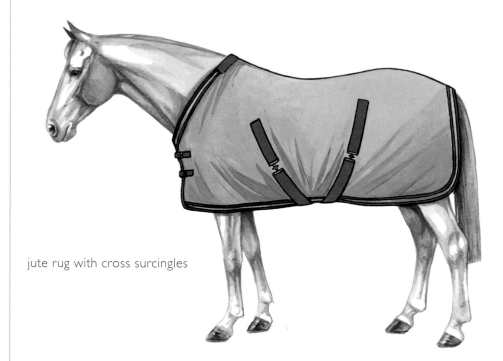

jute rug with cross surcingles

Day rugs

These are traditionally made from good quality 2 lb or 3 lb wool rugging and there is no doubt in my mind that a good quality day rug will keep a horse extremely warm, much warmer than most lightweight quilts. The wool day rug is not, for practical reasons, as easy to maintain as the quilted stable rug made from more manageable modern materials. If you have a day rug with cross surcingles then you eliminate the need to use a roller, which is definitely more comfortable for the horse.

day rug

Quilted under-rugs

These are usually 8 oz or 12 oz and, although cut into the shape of a rug, they are used solely as extra layers for added warmth, so they only have chest fastenings and do not usually have any form of surcingle. This type of rug has a soft wadding inner for warmth and is usually made with a cotton outer, although some quilted under-rugs can be made of breathable nylon.

Quilted under-rugs with necks

These are made on the same principle as the quilted under-rug but have the addition of a neckpiece that is shaped to fold around the horse's neck, usually fastened by Velcro under the neck, and thus covers the horse from just behind the ears to the tail. This type of rug does help to keep down the hair regrowth on the neck after a clip as it is designed to keep the temperature of the horse's neck as warm, or nearly as warm depending on the layers, as the rugged-up body.

quilted under-rug

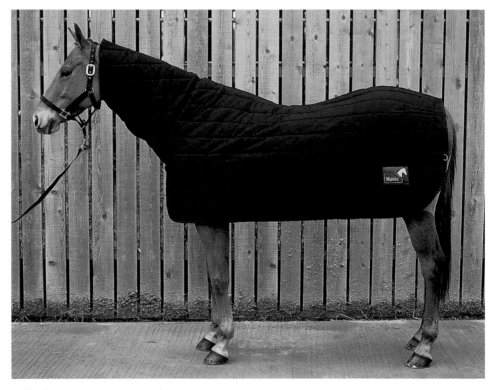

quilted under-rug with neck extension

Woollen under-rugs

A traditional under-rug and, at one time, the only type of under-rug available. The type of clip, stabling or degree of bad weather dictated the number of woollen under-rugs used. Worn under a jute rug, they folded back over the rug and were secured by the roller. As most modern rugs have cross surcingles and no roller, it is not so practical to use a woollen under-rug today.

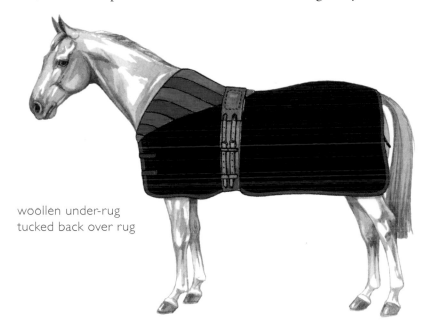

woollen under-rug
tucked back over rug

Summer sheets

These sheets are multi-functional. They provide the horse with a light cover in a horsebox or trailer, where it can get very warm especially in the summer months, and in the stable for summer evenings or to keep the coat neatly laid and dust free. Used as under-rugs in the winter, they keep the underside of your rugs clean as the winter progresses; one on the horse and one in the wash ensures that the horse always has a completely clean rug next to the body. This will also help to keep the coat much cleaner.

TO FIT Just as with a turnout rug, the neckline of a stable rug is crucial to the success of the fit of the rug in the shoulder region. A neckline that is too large for a horse will result in the rug gaping at the front of the shoulders and dropping down so that the neck edging is resting on the points of the shoulders. This will cause severe rubbing and the rug will pull back behind the withers causing pressure sores and rubbing the withers as well. A stable rug can be a

summer sheet

well-fitting stable rug

little shorter than the horse's turnout rug; it should end approximately 2 in in front of the tail so that the horse can raise his tail comfortably. Stable rugs should always have fillet strings on them to help keep them in place as the horse moves about the stable.

The neckline should fit well above the point of shoulder and approximately 2–4 in in front of the withers.

Cross surcingles should be fastened so that there is a hand's breadth between them and the horse's belly.

6

Antirub Vests and Bibs

THERE ARE SEVERAL very good antirub vests and bibs on the market. Bibs are generally made from either a silky material or a cotton quilted outer which is lined with a silky material, and vests are generally made from a stretch material.

A horse's shoulders tend to rub continually against the front of a rug when he moves around the stable or field and when grazing. The constant friction can cause rubbed and even sore places at the point of shoulder and chest on horses with very sensitive skin. If an antirub vest or bib is used, the shoulders have a smooth surface to move against and this helps to prevent hair loss and soreness.

black cotton quilted antirub vest

If your rug is the right size and fits your horse well, he probably will not need an antirub accessory but, if you know that your horse is prone to rubbing, then prevention is better than cure. I have one horse who has a very fine coat and gets rubbed very easily, so now all my horses automatically wear vests all winter.

They are also a good way of preventing the front of your rugs from getting too dirty on the inside. Constantly changing to clean vests or bibs keeps the horse and rug front much cleaner: one bib on and one in the wash for each horse is the easiest way to do this.

TO FIT Vests and bibs are put on over the horse's head and fit snugly over the horse's chest and shoulders reaching as far back as the girth. If you have a problem placing them over the horse's head, try gathering the vest or bib together in both hands so that the material is not as bulky. Stand under the horse's head with your back to his chest; from this position you have more control over the head and are able to stop with the vest or bib resting on the horse's nose if he tries to put his head up. You can gently hold the nose with the vest or bib until the horse is still and then continue to slide it up the face and over his head, and when you have got it over the ears, slide it down the neck to the withers before spreading it out and putting it into place.

Vests fasten at the girth region and bibs, which are shaped like the front of a rug, fasten with a one-loop attachment to the front of the rug. Some vests can cause pressure on the withers so bibs are often the best choice.

nylon antirub vest

7

Hoods (Outdoor and Indoor) and Neck Covers

Outdoor Hoods

These are normally sold to match a particular type of turnout rug. If the hood fits very well, your horse is used to wearing one and you are on a yard with good supervision, then a hood is a useful accessory. It will keep a fully clipped horse warm in severe weather or keep any horse really clean if you do not have a lot of time to spend on grooming sessions prior to exercising. If, however, there is no one available to supervise your horse when he is turned out for long periods of time, then I feel that you should perhaps consider a neck cover instead because some hoods can easily be displaced and cover the horse's eyes which may frighten certain animals.

Neck covers

Neck covers, which also keep the horse's neck warm and clean, leave the face uncovered and are, therefore, in some cases, a safer option than a full hood. Very few full hoods fit the contours of a horse's face perfectly and most, in some way, obscure the horse's vision; with a spooky or sensitive horse this will probably cause an accident.

TO FIT If you are not purchasing a rug that has a neck cover attached, you will need to sew the D rings provided with your hood or neck cover onto the rug so that they can be fastened to the rug securely. It is important that they lie on the outside of the rug so that when it rains the rain runs over them onto the rug and off onto the ground. If a hood or cover is tucked into a rug, the rain will run into the neck of the rug and soak the horse.

The reason that the D rings are not sewn on by the manufacturer is that they

outdoor hood
and rug

could not then genuinely sell the rug as completely waterproof as any stitching sewn through the rug may eventually leak a little.

Outdoor hoods are made of the same material as the rug.

Indoor Hoods

Indoor hoods are useful for a number of reasons, for example they will keep warm a fully clipped horse who really feels the cold, and will preserve the appearance of a glossy summer coat on unclipped native show ponies (shown in their natural state) who have qualified for winter shows.

These hoods are usually made of a very soft smooth material with a high degree of stretch so that the hood fits the contours of the horse's head very well and is not easily displaced. Some hoods can match quilted stable rugs and are made in the same material and thickness to complement the rug.

TO FIT Indoor hoods have quite a variety of fastenings. The quilted type usually fasten under the jaw and neck and have adjustable fittings so that you are able to fit them as closely as possible to the individual horse. The stretch hoods usually either pull on over the horse's head or have a zip fastening under the head and neck. As with any new type of clothing or equipment, introducing things slowly and carefully always pays off in the end. If you know that your horse does not like things put over his head choose a hood that fastens under the head and neck so that you can put it on from the withers and gradually pull it up the neck and then over the head from the body rather than approaching from the front.

Lycra hood on a pony

quilted hood on a pony

8

Coolers

THERE IS A BEWILDERING array of coolers, fleeces and wicking rugs on the market. You must decide what you need the rug to do, or in which situation you will be using it, in order to make the right decision on which one to buy. They can be very expensive, so a rug that the horse is not going to get the full benefit from is going to be a waste of money. These rugs provide the traditional services of cooling horses after work and drying horses after they have been bathed, but modern coolers are also used as travel rugs or as light rugs for day or night before the weather gets cold.

Some of these rugs do not have cross surcingles so you will need to use an elastic surcingle if the horse is to travel in it, and if you are going to use it in the stable for long periods then it will be safer to use a roller and wither pad. If a tail guard is to be attached to an elastic surcingle, make sure the surcingle does not get dragged back by the tail guard; keep the surcingle in place with a breast girth or an old, securely fastened tail bandage.

Some coolers pick up the horse's bedding so, if you are stable proud and do not like your horse to wear his bed all over his rug, try to pick a cooler that does not pick up bedding so easily or be prepared to brush the outside of the rug every day with a finishing brush before taking it off your horse.

Coolers as Stable Rugs

If you want to use a cooler as a day rug, or for long periods in the stable, you need to choose a substantial one or it will simply not stand up to the constant use. Coolers are very stretchy, and do stretch even more over a period of time, it is, therefore, important to buy the right size in the first place. Buy the cooler one size smaller than your horse's normal stable rug size. For example, a horse who normally wears a 6 ft 3 in stable rug will, in most cases, wear a 6 ft cooler.

Coolers as Under-rugs

If the cooler is to be used as an under-rug layer in the winter, it is important that it does not slip back and drag all the other layers back as well; this will not happen if the rug is the correct size. A cooler that is too big will hang out at the back of the layers and drag back even more. The cooler should not be the layer next to the body; putting either a cotton quilted bib, a summer sheet or a light quilt on first will prevent the cooler being dragged back by the horse's movement and his hair.

Types of Cooler

Honeycomb coolers

There are several honeycomb coolers on the market. These rugs have hundreds of little recessed squares giving a honeycombed appearance. They usually have one or two breast straps and cross surcingles and are bound with cotton binding which helps to minimize excess stretching. They are made of a cotton and acrylic mix which wicks moisture from the horse's skin through the rug to the outside where it lies as a sort of fine mist on top of the fabric until it evaporates.

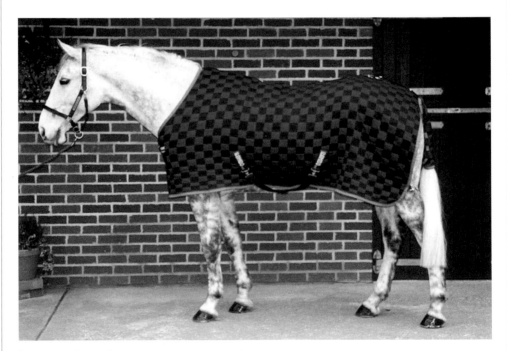

honeycomb cooler

Polar fleece coolers

These rugs really hug the contours of the horse's body and, like most coolers, are multi-purpose. They wick moisture away from a wet or a sweating horse and allow his body to breathe. They are useful travelling rugs or night rugs when the weather can be very changeable in the spring. The fleece material is very stretchy so it is important to buy a rug of the correct size for your horse and then to make sure it is well made enough to stand up to the job you want it to do.

polar fleece cooler

Luddenden coolers

This type of cooler is made from a soft wicking fabric that allows moisture from the horse's skin to pass through the rug and quickly evaporate from the outside of the rug. It is well cut to fit the horse's shape and has cross surcingles that make it more practical for general use than those without cross surcingles.

TO FIT Coolers are usually made from a stretch material and you will, therefore, probably find you need to buy your cooler one size smaller than the size your horse would normally wear in a stable rug. Coolers with a wide neck opening will probably stretch back and sit behind the withers, pulling and rubbing on the shoulders. Try to pick a rug with a neckline that fits into the

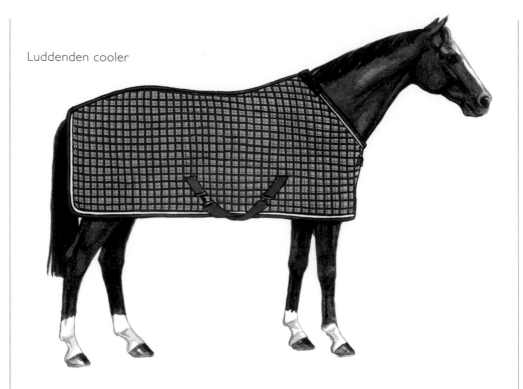

Luddenden cooler

horse's neck on the line in front of the withers where the neck meets the shoulders, and that has good chest fastenings. The neckline should, preferably, be bound with a nonstretch binding.

Thermatex multi-purpose rugs
These rugs are made from three breathable layers. The insulating layer traps air just like the horse's own coat. The inner layer of wool has excellent wicking capabilities. The middle layer of polypropylene keeps the layers apart so that the moisture cannot get back to the horse. The moisture, water or sweat, is driven upwards by the combined action of the wicking properties of the wool layer and the warmth of the horse's body. Then, like the honeycomb coolers, the moisture lies on top of the rug in a fine mist until it evaporates leaving the horse dry and warm under the rug.

TO FIT It is most important that you get the right size for your horse or pony. You will need to buy at least a size smaller than your horse normally wears in a stable rug. If, for instance, your horse normally wears a 6 ft 3 in stable rug then he will need a 6 ft Thermatex rug. As a guide, one of my own ponies wears a

5 ft 9 in turnout rug, a 5 ft 6 in stable rug and a 5 ft 3 in Thermatex. The Thermatex rugs come with two substantial chest fastenings and either a single belly strap or cross surcingles. I have never found the need for anything other than the single belly strap as the rug never slips. Make sure that both the chest straps are fastened properly and that the belly strap is done up snugly into the horse's belly at girth level.

Thermatex SHR rug

9

Travelling Your Horse

THE OLD SAYING, 'prevention is better than cure', definitely applies to what your horse wears to travel in. In the awful event of an accident your horse has a better chance of surviving unscathed if he is adequately and properly protected. Even if you never have an accident, a cut or knock sustained while going up or down the ramp, or if you have to brake suddenly while travelling, can injure your horse and stop you being able to compete when a better set of travel boots or a tail guard would have prevented the injury in the first place.

Travel Boots

Travel boots are definitely the quickest and easiest form of leg protection but, if you are going to invest in these boots, it is essential that you get a well-made set. The cheaper versions tend to be a little short, especially on the bigger types of horses, and they really need to be substantially made so that they keep their rigidity and do not slide down the horse's legs.

Travel boots must cover the horse from just above the knee on the forelegs and just above the hock on the hind legs and must also come low enough so that the whole of the coronory band and the bulbs of the heels are well protected. When you look in catalogues you continually see travel boots advertised that leave the whole of the coronary band and the horse's heels exposed and these are areas that are easily damaged by the horse treading on himself or stepping onto or off the ramp badly.

TO FIT Place each boot on the horse and do the Velcro up from the top to the bottom of the boot. Then retighten each individual Velcro fastening in turn to make sure it is secure. Make sure the boot is well wrapped around the horse's leg and that it fits snugly against the leg. As the boots are so bulky it is very

Foxi completely prepared for travel

well-fitting front travel
boots

difficult to get them too tight but, as a guide, you should be able to get two fingers comfortably down between the boots and the horse's leg.

Travel Bandages

If you decide to use travel bandages, the best sort of padding to go under them is the shaped Fybagee pads which come just above the hock on the hind leg and just above the knee on the foreleg. These come in sets of four pads in pony, cob and full sizes. Make sure the bandages you use are long enough for your horse. Bandages of 3 m in length will do for the average horse and pony but larger horses will need 4 m long bandages to ensure they will be long enough to cover the whole area. The sort of bandage you use should be either stretch jersey, fastened with tapes or Velcro, or polo-type bandages made of Polatec or polo fleece. There are companies that specialise in bandages for miniature horses but if you are bandaging an average small pony just cut off a little of the bandage so that you do not have to go up and down the legs of an 11 hh pony more than twice!

TO FIT When the pad is in place on the leg, pull it as firmly as you can so that the pad closes around the horse's leg and overlaps at the edges. Then, without releasing the pressure, start bandaging from just under the knee or hock, band-aging and closing the pad as you work your way down the horse's leg. Try to

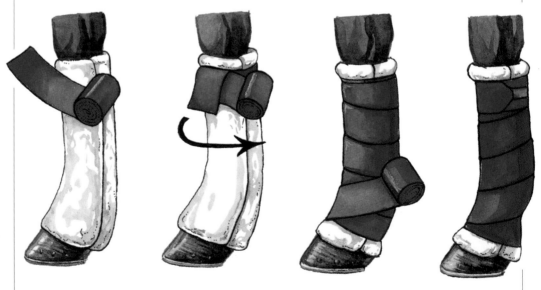

how to apply travel bandages

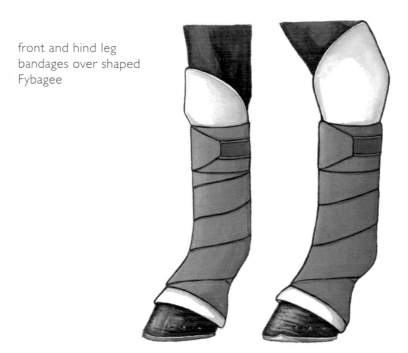

front and hind leg bandages over shaped Fybagee

keep the bandaging even all the way down and back up the leg, this will help to keep the pressure evenly distributed. Bandage right over the fetlock and onto the pastern making sure that the pad covers the coronary band and the bulbs of the heel. Carry on bandaging back up the leg until you come to the end of the bandage. Try to make sure that the fastening of the bandage ends up on the outside of the horse's leg and does not end up knotted or tightly Velcroed over the tendon area.

Knee Boots

If you just want to bandage from below the knee then you can use knee boots to protect the knee area. They come in a variety of materials from neoprene to blanketing and leather, and are designed to prevent the horse from damaging the front of the knee joint if he should fall on his knees.

TO FIT It is very important that the top strap is done up firmly so that the boot cannot slip off the knee and end up around the horse's lower joints and be trodden on. Contrary to that, the bottom strap must be loose so that the horse can bend his knee and so that no pressure is put on the back of the knee joint because this is an area that is easily damaged.

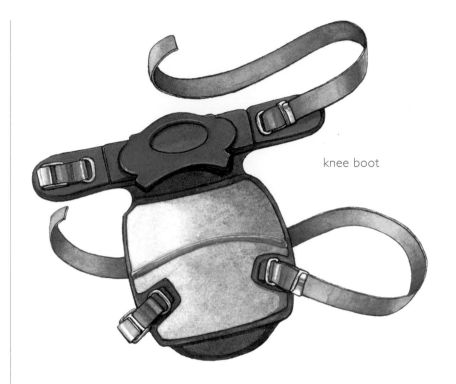

knee boot

a pair of knee
boots

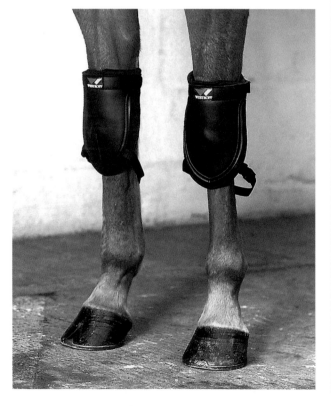

Hock Boots

As with knee boots, if you just want to bandage the hind leg from just under the hock to the coronary band then hock boots will protect the point of the hock in particular. This area is very easily rubbed or injured when a horse maintains his balance when travelling by sitting back on the tail and hind-quarters to brace himself.

TO FIT Again, as with knee boots, it is important that the top strap is done up firmly so that the boot does not slip down but not so tightly that it impairs the horse's circulation, especially on a long journey. You should just be able to get one finger comfortably between the top strap and the horse's leg. The bottom strap should allow enough movement so the horse can comfortably bend the hind leg to walk up and down the ramp and to move comfortably.

hock boot

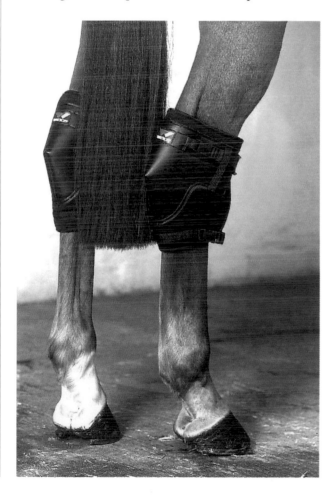

a pair of hock boots

Tail Bandages

The idea of bandaging the tail is to protect the dock which is the end of the horse's spine. Make sure you bandage from the very top of the tail to just below where the bone ends so that the whole of the dock is protected. The tail should not be bandaged tightly for long periods of time and a stretch bandage should never be put on wet as it will tighten as it dries and stop the circulation in the tail.

TO FIT It is very important to get the bandage neat, even and of the same pressure all the way down. A lot of serious damage has been caused to tails and legs by bad bandaging. Bandage from the top to the bottom of the dock and make sure the fastening tapes are flat and even; when you do them up they should not cut into the tail but apply the same pressure as the rest of the bandage. If you are using a mane and tail spray it is a good idea not to spray the very top of the tail before you put on a tail bandage as this makes the top of the tail very shiny and slippery which makes the tail bandage slip down. Just apply spray to the tail below the dock so that the bottom of the tail looks nice.

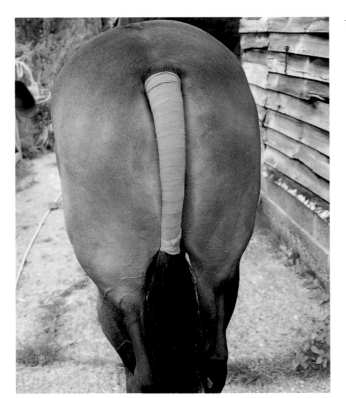

tail bandage in place

Tail Guards

These are normally used in addition to a tail bandage for further protection. There are several tail guards that stay up on their own so they do not need to be attached to a rug. As a lot of rugs are fastened by cross surcingles instead of rollers these days, it is an important thing to take into consideration. If it is hot and your horse will not be wearing a rug when travelling then, again, you need a tail guard that stays up by itself.

TO FIT Lift the tail so that you can get the tail guard up to the top of the dock. Place the guard under the tail so that it will do up on the top of the tail not underneath. Make sure that it is fastened securely and firmly so that it will not come off in transit, but not so tight that it is cutting into the horse.

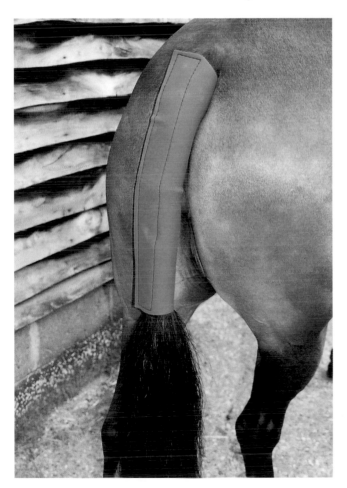

neoprene tail guard

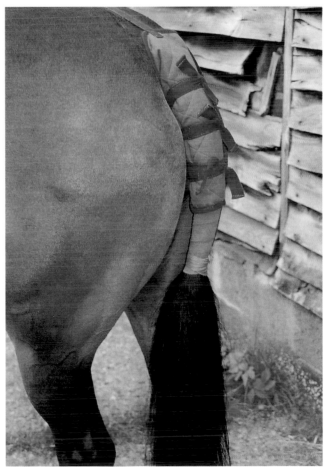

cotton quilted tied tail guard

Poll Guards

There are two types of poll guard. One is simply a thick, padded sausage-shaped 'bumper' that lies across the poll and attaches to the headcollar. The other type sits right over the top of the head like a cap, fitting over the ears and also attaching to the headcollar.

Travelling Youngstock

Older, experienced horses are used to, and can cope with, travel boots and numerous travel accessories but youngstock who have not been handled very much need the maximum protection from the minimum amount of equipment. Soft Polotec bandages are the ideal solution. They can be applied straight on the legs without padding. The only extra protection required is a tail bandage.

A weanling travelling to his first show alone will be best left untied in a trailer with all the partitions removed. The trailer should have a good nonslip surface and a generous layer of bedding. Youngsters normally travel facing the rear with their legs splayed slightly which helps them to find their balance more easily.

10

Numnahs, Saddle Squares and Back Pads

MOST OF US THESE days use some sort of numnah, saddle square or pad under our saddles, whether it is a light cotton quilt just to keep the underneath of the saddle clean, or something much thicker for a specific purpose.

All numnahs, saddle squares and pads must be fitted correctly; they should be placed forward on the horse's back and then slid back in the direction of hair growth to ensure that the hair lies flat. They must be lifted into the gullet of the saddle and not press on the horse's spine.

Numnahs

Numnahs are pads in the shape of the saddle and come in a variety of different materials and thicknesses. There are three slightly differing shapes: the general purpose numnah is forward cut to fit the shape of the GP saddle flap; the working hunter numnah is cut a little straighter to accommodate the shape of a working hunter saddle and the dressage numnah is cut even straighter to follow the line of the straight-cut front thigh roll of a dressage saddle. Today numnahs come in many colours and you can colour co-ordinate your bandages with the numnah, and the binding around the numnah's edge can be in a contrasting colour. Generally, numnahs for competition use are white, black or brown and working hunter numnahs should always be brown to match the brown show tack.

TO FIT The numnah must be slightly bigger than the saddle it is to go under so that the saddle does not press down on the seams of the binding that goes all around the edge of the numnah which will cause pressure sores on the horse's back. As you place the saddle over the numnah you must lift the numnah up into the gullet of the saddle before girthing up the saddle so that there is no pressure on the horse's spine. The strap at the front of the numnah loops around, and is fastened to, one of the saddle's girth straps under the flap on each side before the saddle is girthed up. The girth passes through a loop at the bottom of the numnah just under the panel of the saddle.

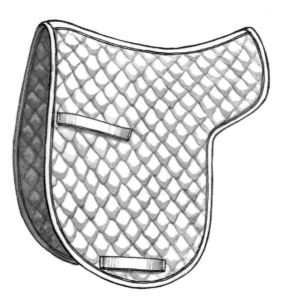

cotton quilted dressage numnah

GP numnah

Saddle Squares

This type of saddle pad is also designed to either keep the saddle clean or to afford extra padding for the horse in differing degrees but, instead of being saddle shaped, these pads are almost square. This shape means that more of the pad is visible so they are popular for either colour co-ordination purposes or for displaying initials in the corner of the square. Dressage competitors can have their competition number pouches sewn onto the corner of the square so that they can show the numbers for each class.

TO FIT The saddle square must, again, be slightly bigger than the saddle so that the saddle does not rest on any of the seams of the saddle square and cause a pressure point or a sore on the horse's back. The square should be pulled well up into the gullet of the saddle before being girthed up. The strap at the front of the saddle square loops around, and is fastened to, one of the saddle's girth straps under the flap on each side before the saddle is girthed up. The girth passes through a loop at the bottom of the saddle square just under the panel of the saddle.

saddle square

Gel and Back Pads

There are dozens of gel pads and back pads on the market. The most important point to remember is that they must be sufficiently thick to actually be of some use. If you squeeze the pad between your thumbnail and your index fingernail the gel should not part so that you can feel your fingernails meet. They must be of good quality so that they do not deteriorate when they are washed or in day-to-day use thus spreading the bearing load unevenly and causing the sort of trouble they are designed to help prevent.

TO FIT They must be pliable so that they fit very well and if they are not shaped to fit up into the gullet of the saddle they must be pliable enough to be pulled well up into the gullet so there is no downward pressure onto the spine. To extend the life of a gel pad it is better not to have it placed directly on the horse's back because this would mean washing the pad more frequently. If you have a light quilted square next to the horse with the gel pad on top, you will extend the life of the pad.

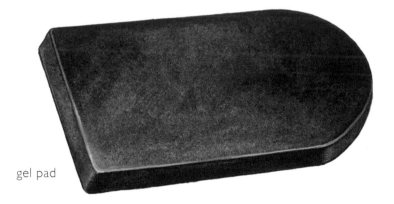

gel pad

Argentine Saddle Blankets

A traditional cotton-mix woven oblong saddle blanket with a fringe on each end. Designed to be worn under polo ponies' saddles, they come in a vast range of colours and can be specially ordered in team colours but, if required for a specific date, you must give your retailer enough warning as they can take weeks to be made and then shipped from the Argentine. These blankets are not very easy to maintain as the colours can run if washed in too hot a wash. Because they are worn folded in two they only cover the area under the bearing surface of the saddle and because a polo saddle has only a half panel and very small sweat flaps, the girth buckle can end up on the pony's skin causing sores. It is better to use a polo blanket in conjunction with another form of saddle pad to give the pony more protection.

TO FIT This blanket should be worn folded over so that there is a double thickness next to the pony and it should be pulled well up into the gullet of the saddle to prevent the saddle pushing the pad down and putting undue pressure on the spine. Because polo is such a fast sport and the ponies sweat freely, it is important that, in order to prevent sore backs, the pads are kept very clean but not washed in too harsh a detergent. The ponies must always have a clean blanket to wear.

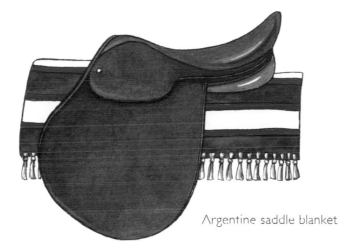

Argentine saddle blanket

Driving-saddle Pads

These pads fit under driving-harness saddles to prevent pressure or sore places on the horse's back. This is particularly important for a sensitive-skinned horse.

TO FIT The pad has Velcro fastenings that fasten the pad securely to the driving saddle to stop it slipping, one under the gullet and one each side of the pad. It should be placed under the driving saddle and pulled up into the gullet of the saddle before the Velcro is fastened and before the driving saddle is girthed up.

Riser Pads

Riser pads are dense foam pads shaped to fit neatly under the bearing surface of the saddle and up into the gullet so that no pressure is brought to bear directly on the horse's spine. Ideally, all horses' saddles should fit them perfectly but there are those horses who present a number of saddle-fitting problems.

PolyPad driving Rollerpad shown with the PolyPad breast collar pad

Riser pads provide the means for the slight adjustment that can make a horse comfortable in his work. These pads should not, however, be used just to make a badly made saddle fit a horse. They have three different degrees of thickness and uses.

The ordinary riser is the same thickness all the way along the pad and is designed to give even, comfortable padding under the bearing surface of the saddle.

The front riser is the same thickness as the ordinary riser but has extra padding at the front so that the saddle is lifted at the front a little.

The back riser is, as the name suggests, the opposite to the front riser. It has the same dense padding all the way along but extra at the back in order to lift the saddle at the back.

TO FIT The pad should be placed under the saddle so that the saddle fits comfortably in the middle of the pad and does not overlap the pad. The pad should fit well up into the gullet of the saddle. As this is a dense foam pad, the horse does tend to sweat under it if it is placed directly next to the horse so it would be better sandwiched between the saddle and a light quilted numnah or saddle square. All the layers must be well pulled up into the gullet of the saddle before the saddle is girthed up.

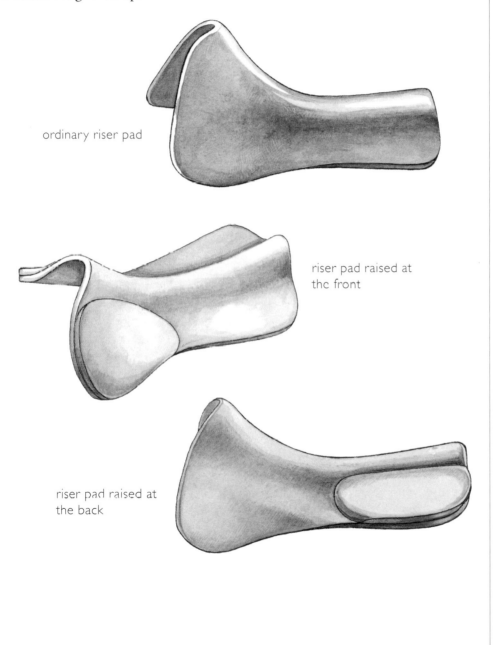

ordinary riser pad

riser pad raised at the front

riser pad raised at the back

PolyPads

These rectangular saddle pads come in several thicknesses and are very easy to maintain as the pad outer is cotton and the inner is washable wadding. Designed not to move if fitted properly and pulled well up into the gullet of the saddle, they do not have any loops or fittings, which can be a little unnerving if you are used to securing conventional numnahs and squares. They come in various colours and bindings so they can be co-ordinated with personal and team colours very easily.

TO FIT Place the PolyPad forward on the horse's back and slide it back into position. Place the saddle on top so that there is approximately 3 in of pad sticking out at the front and 2 in sticking out at the back of the saddle. Then hold the pad with one hand at the front over the horse's spine and one hand at the back and lift the pad right up into the gullet of the saddle so that there is a gap over the horse's spine, then girth up the saddle as normal.

PolyPad

11

Fly Masks, Nose Nets and Fly and Midge Rugs

IF YOU HAVE A HORSE who is prone to sweet itch, or is very sensitive to flies landing on him, or is a head shaker, or is sun sensitive, you are very unfortunate. There is no simple solution to any of these but there are quite a few ways in which we can help to improve a horse's quality of life. It really is worth trying out several forms of additives and masking techniques plus, perhaps, night turnout (after the midges have gone to bed and before they get up again) instead of day turnout, as different horses have responded very favourably to various forms of help.

Fly Masks

A fly mask has to be made of fairly substantial fine netting in order to withstand the rough usage it will get. It is much safer and better if your mask fits your horse without needing a headcollar to keep it on as there is less risk of your horse getting caught up on a fence; a headcollar may not break whereas the mask will either come unfastened or break in an emergency.

TO FIT The mask should be well shaped so that there is plenty of room for the horse's eyes to open and close without touching the mask. If you choose a mask with ears, this will ensure one less place for flies to land and cause irritation. The mask should fit securely to the head with no obvious gaps to allow flies to crawl in and should fasten firmly under the face without causing any rubbed places. For some months your horse might have to wear a mask every time he is turned out, so it must fit comfortably and well.

fly mask with ears

Fly fringes

Some fringes rely on a headcollar to keep them in place. If you have one of these make sure that you have an inexpensive web headcollar or a leather one; both will break if your horse should become hooked up on anything in the field. There are a few versions of fringes on the market that loop over the ears and do not have to be worn with a headcollar at all. Do not wash several fly fringes together as they become knotted together and cannot be used again! Fly fringes do give relief to horses who have sensitive eyes and react badly to flies constantly landing on and around their eye area.

TO FIT If you are using a fringe that is held on by a headcollar, fit it just as you would fit a browband. The fly fringe should be long enough to allow the forehead plenty of room and not drag the headcollar forward chafing the back of the horse's ears. The fringe should reach well below the horse's eyes in order to protect them properly.

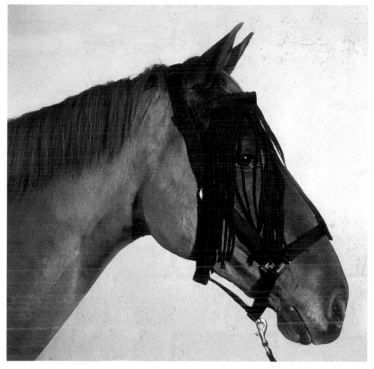

fly fringe

cotton fly veil

Fly veils

Fly veils are crocheted out of cotton with plain cotton ear protection. These veils can be very useful as they keep flies from landing on the horse's ears and if they are sprayed with fly spray before you put them on the horse's head they help to keep flies away from the horse's face in general.

TO FIT These veils only come in one size so, if you are putting one on a small animal, you will need to turn the ears inside out and stitch around them to make them a little smaller, then cut off the excess. Veils fit over the ears and hang down to the eyes fastening with a single piece of cord at the throat where the throatlash of the bridle fastens. For extra security wind the cord around the bridle throatlash to keep it from getting caught up in any other item of tack.

Nose nets

A nose net should be made from as fine a netting as possible and have good attachments to enable you to fit it securely and easily to the noseband of your bridle. The nets reduce the amount of pollen breathed in through the horse's nostrils so lowering the level of irritation that might cause the horse to sneeze or to inflame the membranes causing him to headshake.

TO FIT Make sure the net is big enough to fit the horse's muzzle and that the horse is still able to open his mouth enough to be able to relax his jaw. Secure the tapes of the nose net to the noseband of the bridle with the Velcro fastenings. As the nose net is constantly over the horse's mouth and constantly getting wet it is probably better to have two, one on and one in the wash. It is most important to keep them clean as the horse can so easily be rubbed by a dirty nose net.

nose net attached to the noseband of a bridle

Turnout Fly Rugs

These rugs need to be very tough to be able to withstand everything a horse does when turned out in a field but also need to be of fine mesh to allow a good circulation of air on a hot day and also protect the horse from fly irritation. They give very good protection from UV sunlight and help to stop the horse's coat from bleaching. These rugs are not ideal for horses or ponies with sweet itch as the holes are not really small enough to stop midges from biting. Also, unless the rug has a large belly flap the midges can simply fly under the edge of the rug and bite the horse on his underside. As with all these protective measures, you need to start using them early. It is too late if the animal has already started to rub and the itching is at an advanced stage because they will rub with the rug on and destroy it. You need to begin all protective measures a good month before prime fly and midge time including feed additives and other forms of protection.

TO FIT In general, a turnout rug will probably need to be 3 in bigger than a horse's stable rug to allow plenty of freedom of movement. Make sure the cross surcingles are done up snugly so that the rug wraps under the belly area a little

Rambo Flybuster rug complete with fly mask

and that the neck and fly mask fit snugly to the face and neck. Check carefully and regularly for rubbed places, particularly at the shoulder region, as some meshes can be abrasive for horses with sensitive skin. You may even have to consider a lightweight silky bib to help protect the horse's shoulders.

Net Fly Rugs

These rugs are made of very fine netting, so fine that even the tiniest insect will find it very difficult to actually land on the horse's skin. They come with a neck cover made of the same material to protect as much of the horse as possible and, when combined with a matching fly mask, will go a long way to helping very sensitive-skinned horses. The only real drawback is that these rugs are very soft and fine and will not stand up to any really rough use. They should only be used outside under strict supervision, then, for any period of time your horse is turned out in a paddock, use electric fencing so that there is nothing for him to rub the rug on, this will help to keep the rug whole for a longer period of time.

TO FIT Fly rugs should fit so that the horse has plenty of freedom of movement and the neck cover, if not directly attached to the rug, should clip securely

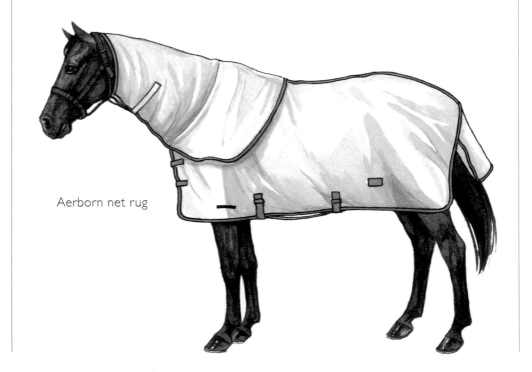

Aerborn net rug

into place so that as the horse lowers his head to eat or graze the cover stays neatly against the rug. If the cover slides down towards the horse's head it will irritate him or obscure his vision or cause an accident by becoming unfastened.

Boett Blankets

The Boett Blanket has been specially designed to combat the distressing and disfiguring effects of sweet itch. It does look a little like horse pyjamas but has proved to be extremely effective. This rug was designed in Sweden ten years ago to protect horses and ponies who have allergies to insect bites. The Blanket is made from a light very durable fabric that midges are unable to bite through. It is constructed so that all the areas that are most affected by sweet itch are very well covered. Ideally a horse or pony who is prone to sweet itch should begin to wear this rug before any symptoms appear. Past experience of any horse or pony you have owned for a number of years should give you an indication of when to expect irritations to begin. Try to start using rugs, masks and any food additives at least a month before. This will help to stop things happening in the first place and vastly reduce the disfiguring effect. But even after the sweet itch starts this rug can make a tremendous difference. The sores and irritation will heal, the skin will begin to go back to normal and hair regrowth will start.

TO FIT The Blanket itself is an all-in-one outfit with complete neck coverage with a long line body rug and tail flap. The rug is slipped on over the horse's or pony's head and there is an elastic neckband that adjusts behind the ears to ensure a snug fit. The rug fits as a conventional one would but has a wider-than-normal bellyband which covers most of the underbelly area. It is made of a stretch material so it is very important to get the right advice from the UK agent as to what size your particular horse or pony will need. It has the added advantages of being made in sizes right down the scale to fit really small ponies as well.

Boett hoods
This hood is designed to be used in conjunction with the Boett Blanket. Made of the same material, this hood affords as much protection to the head as possible. In some cases of sweet itch, only the mane and forelock area are affected but in very severe cases the face, and particularly the eye area, can be seriously affected.

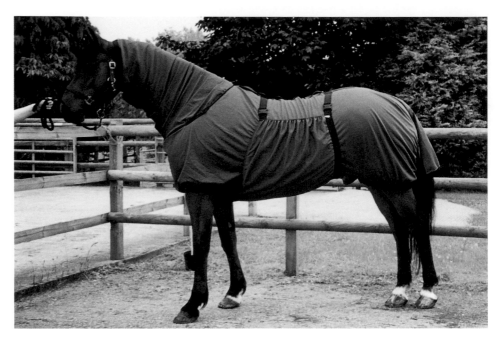

the Boett Blanket has veterinary endorsement as a sweet-itch treatment

Boett sweet-itch face hood

TO FIT The hood caters for a lot of adjustment and fits the face snugly. It is secured to the rug by a loop just behind the ears and a long elastic strap which is fastened to a point just inside the Blanket at the withers area. No headcollar is required. Let your horse or pony get used to wearing his hood in a stable or safe place several times before being turned out in it. Make sure a hood fits very well and does not obscure the horse's vision so that he will not be afraid when turned out in the paddock or field for the first time with one on.

12

Boots and Bandages

FOR ANY FORM OF schooling you need to think about protection and/or support for the horse's legs. It will depend on the type of schooling or work you intend to do, and on the age, fitness and health of your horse as to which type of boot or bandage is going to be most suitable. It is far better to spend a little time and money on a good pair of brushing boots than footing yet another vet's bill for an injury that could have been so easily prevented.

One of the most important things to remember if you are using boots or bandages is that not only must the horse's legs be scrupulously clean and free from veterinary products, but so must any boot or bandage that is put on them. Any boot or bandage that is dirty will cause sores and rubbed places. The majority of brushing boots are made of some form of nylon or neoprene, both materials tend to make the surface they cover heat up and sweat. A lot of medicinal cooling and healing products specifically list in their information that they either should not be covered or that they should not be tightly bandaged. It is most important if you have a horse who is in work but needs a supportive boot or bandage and also some sort of medicinal product applied, that you apply the product correctly and stick to the recommended guidelines. Remove all trace of the product before you put on a neoprene boot in particular.

Boots

Brushing boots

In order to be effective, brushing boots must meet certain standards or it really is not worth putting them on the horse's legs. The base material must be thick enough to actually afford some protection. The inner pad that runs down the leg has to be a good shape in order to cover the inside of the leg and also to cup the inner part of the fetlock joint. The hind boots should, preferably, have a larger padded area over the fetlock joint as some horses brush continually at the back on the lower half of the joint. The materials used must be pliable and mould to the shape of the leg. The boot should be long enough to cover the whole area from just under the knee to just below the fetlock and the hind boots should be longer than the front boots because the hind cannon bones are longer than the front cannon bones in the majority of horses. Brushing boots should have an easy but secure and effective fastening.

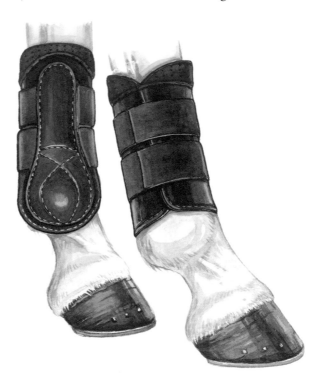

brushing boot showing inner area

Tendon boots

There are various tendon boot designs; you need to choose the one that suits your purpose best. If you need a tendon boot to protect the tendons of a jumping horse then an open-fronted boot will leave the front of the horse's legs exposed and ensure he remains sensitive to knocked poles while protecting the tendons from being struck at the back by the toes of the hind feet. Polo ponies require a much more substantial boot to go over polo bandages to give hind-foot-strike protection, protection from other horses during riding off and protection from a blow by a polo mallet. Make sure that the boots you buy are well made and substantial enough to do the job you require, and that the fastenings are well made and fasten properly and safely.

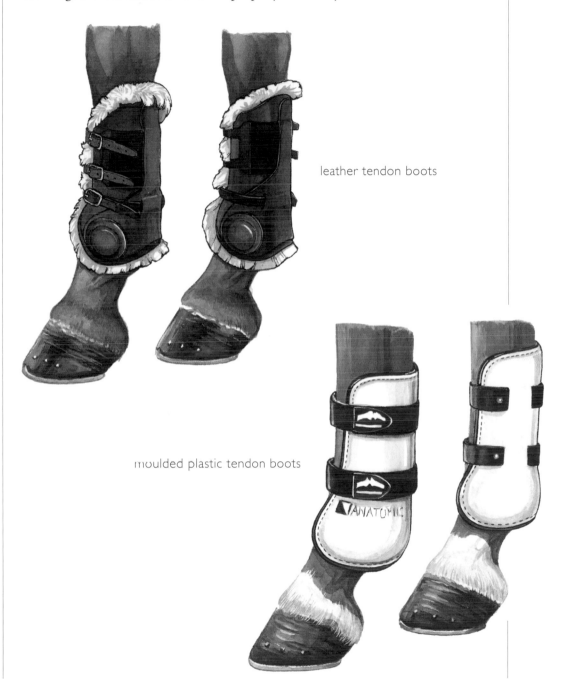

leather tendon boots

moulded plastic tendon boots

Speedy-cut boots

A speedy-cut injury often occurs when fast work is being carried out, it is an unusually high cut just under either the knee or hock. The boot is a brushing boot that is cut much longer and higher than a conventional brushing boot which extends the area covered to protect the lower knee and hock. Again, they must be well made and mould to the leg staying firmly in place during any fast galloping or jumping work.

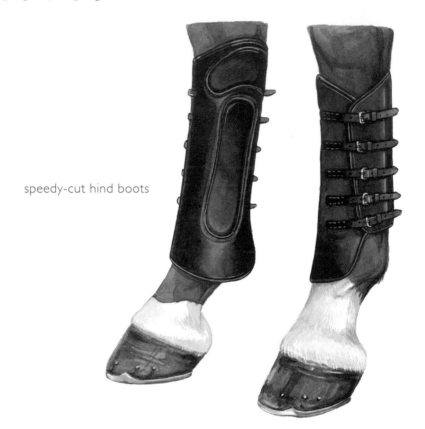

speedy-cut hind boots

Professional's Choice sports medicine boots

These boots were designed for the performance horse or pony, they give exceptional protection and support and should be used for specific purposes. The boots warm the horse's legs, creating a moist environment that enhances blood circulation, and support and protect the legs from side impact and concussion. They can be used on horses who are sound and competing in rigorous conditions such as cross-country jumping or FEI carriage marathons or for fast schooling work or prolonged trotting on the roads. Most of our time with horses is spent in preparation for competition and not actually competing so it makes sense to protect and support the legs so that we can actually get to the event with a sound horse. They are also very good boots for a horse who has had an injury and is being brought back into work and for older horses with weaknesses. They may also prevent yet another call to the vet by protecting the legs of those horses who are inclined to tear recklessly around their paddocks.

It is important to get the sizing right, as with all boots, and if you are looking for a high degree of proven protection and support make sure you buy the correct boot and not a lookalike. For horses with long hind cannon bones there is a high-top version that is 2 in longer than the standard boot. It is also very important that you follow the manufacturers' recommended guide lines particularly when fitting, as a badly fitting boot can be worse than no boot at all.

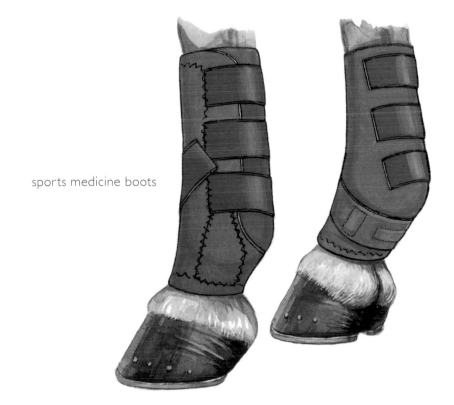

sports medicine boots

Skid boots

Specifically designed to protect the ergot and the underneath of the hind fetlock joint, skid boots are mostly used for the training and working of ridden Western horses and polo ponies. These horses use sliding halts in their work which means that, as they halt or turn in a fast gait, the joints are under so much pressure that they are actually pushed into and slide along the ground. The boots are made of thick neoprene with a thickly covered inner brushing pad and an extra rubber pad covering the lower fetlock area cupping the back and the underside of the fetlock joint. New versions now bend under the horse's ergot and extend at the back to wrap around the upper back pastern area so that no dirt can slide into the boots as a polo pony or a reining horse slides to a halt.

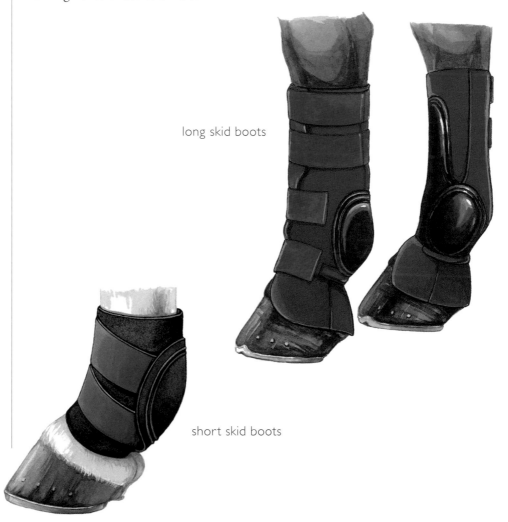

long skid boots

short skid boots

Combination boots

These incorporate a brushing boot and a bell boot all in one boot. Some versions do not allow for enough freedom of movement but Professional's Choice have designed a hinged version that does not inhibit any movement. This is the ultimate in all-round protection. You need to make sure the boot is firmly secured around the leg so that it does not slip down as that will cause the bell boot to be pushed lower on the foot as well. It is possible for a pony to tread on and be brought down by a boot that is too big or has slipped down. Although the boot should be wrapped firmly round the horse's leg you should be able to get an index finger comfortably into the boot at the top.

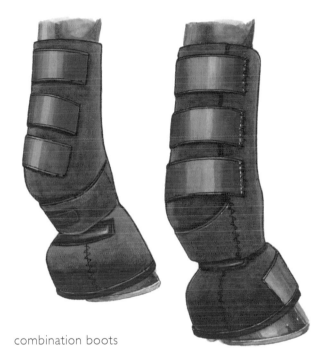

combination boots

Fetlock boots

Designed to protect the fetlock area on the hind legs, fetlock boots are most commonly seen on jumping horses. They come in a variety of materials from neoprene to leather, some with neoprene or sheepskin removable inner pieces. They protect only the inner fetlock joint, so, if your horse is prone to brushing elsewhere on the hind limbs, you really need to have a full brushing boot instead.

fetlock boots

Overreach boots

Also called bell boots, these boots are specifically designed to protect the coronary band and the bulbs of the heels. They are usually worn only on the front legs but can be worn all round in, for instance, the marathon section of carriage driving trials as extra protection is often needed, particularly when more than one horse is being driven. A horse in the wheel of a carriage (the horse closest to the front of a carriage) can often overstep and catch the heels on the hind legs of the lead horse in front of him. Overreach boots on the hind feet of your lead horses can, therefore, prevent these heel injuries. The ordinary overreach boots, either the pull-on version or those with tab or Velcro fastenings, all give very good protection against overreach wounds caused by the horse striking himself but the padded bell boot also gives a high degree of protection against treads received from the close proximity of other horses, as in the game of polo for instance.

Sausage boots

A sausage boot is a piece of dense rubber tubing with a leather strap running through the middle which is fastened around the horse's back pastern on one hind leg only. They are used for a horse who continually brushes in one place, just marking the coronary band on one hind leg, for example, each time it is worked.

tab overreach boots

bell boots

Velcro overreach boots

rubber overreach boots

sausage boot

Pastern wraps

This boot is a neoprene wrap that literally just wraps around the pastern and covers the horse's leg with one layer in this vulnerable area. It is extremely useful for those horses who constantly manage to injure themselves between the top of an overreach boot and the bottom of a brushing boot.

pastern wrap

Bandages

Exercise bandages

Exercise bandages are elastic bandages that come in 3 in or 4 in widths and in a large variety of colours. They should be put on very evenly and firmly and always put on over Gamgee or Fybagee. Tapes should be flat and only as tight as the bandage, no tighter, the knot should be on the outside of the leg and, to ensure they remain safely fastened, either sewn or bandage-taped into place. Some exercise bandages can also be fastened with a Velcro tie-back, again the Velcro tape must only be as tight as the bandage itself and the metal staple must be on the outside of the leg.

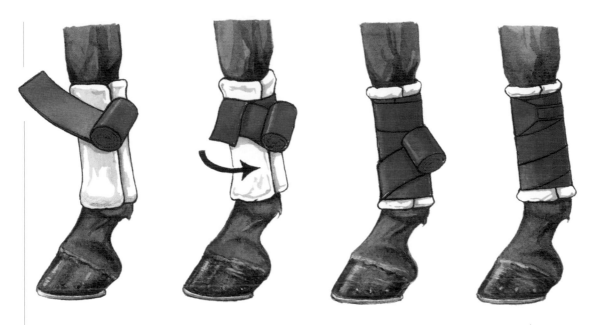

how to apply an exercise bandage

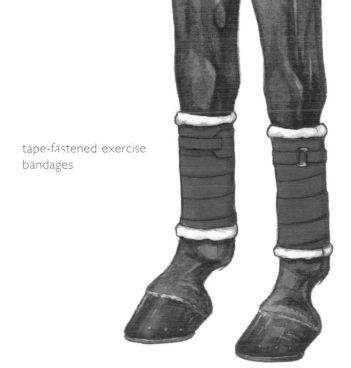

tape-fastened exercise
bandages

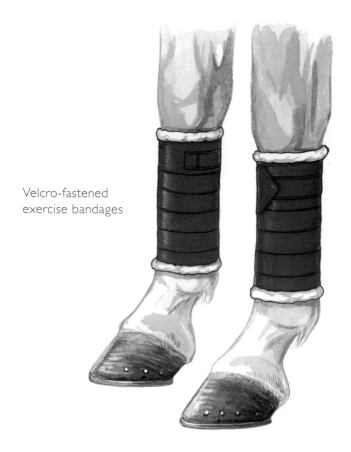

Velcro-fastened
exercise bandages

Polo bandages

These come in a wide variety of colours and are designed to be bandaged
directly onto the horse's leg. They are made of soft stretchy Polatec and mould
to the shape of the leg as you bandage. They can be used to just cover the
cannon bone and upper fetlock area or to bandage lower to cover the fetlock
joint as well. They are very useful for supportive protection for extravagant
youngsters as you can bandage down to the pastern and then meet the bottom
of the bandage with overreach boots. When used for polo, the pony will need
additional protection in the form of skid boots over the bandages on the hind
legs and tendon or heavy brushing boots on the front legs plus bell boots on
the front hooves to prevent the heels being trodden on.

TO FIT You need to make sure all boots and bandages are applied correctly
and very securely so that they will never come undone and cause an accident.
As a general rule you should be able to fit your index finger comfortably into
the top of any boot or bandage, they should be the same tension all the way

down the legs and any fastening should only be as tight as the boot or bandage itself, no tighter, because this creates a tighter band that digs into the leg.

Never fasten bandages over the tendon area as you are liable to cause damage to this very vulnerable part of the horse's leg.

polo bandages on the front legs

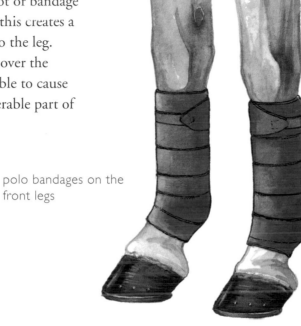

13

Exercise Rugs and Reflective Wear

Driving Exercise Rugs

The very best driving exercise rugs are designed so that you can take them on and off without having to remove any part of the harness and you can go at any gait and in any weather without the rug moving. They need to be cut shorter than the ordinary exercise rug so that they just fit the horse from directly behind the driving pad to just where the dock joins the back strap. The best materials are those that mould to the shape of the horse so that there is no likelihood of the rug filling with air and flapping to frighten him.

TO FIT After you have harnessed your horse, but just before you put the bridle and reins on, place the exercise rug onto the horse's back just behind the pad and thread the top Velcro strap around the gullet of the pad. Then, thread the straps on each side (which are situated approximately at the level of the tugs on a single driving pad) around the pad. The rug has a fillet string so that it cannot blow up in a gust of wind and you must make sure the fillet is tight enough so that it does not rest between the breeching seat and the horse's quarters because, if it does, it will rub him. The rug can easily be put on and removed without having to undo or take off any harness and is secure at all times.

Wool and Melton Exercise Rugs

These rugs are for warmth only and will not keep your horse dry. They are very useful for a fully clipped horse who feels the cold on a raw day in winter. Wool and Witney exercise blankets are usually made of 2 lb rugging material and are the warmest exercise rugs available. Melton exercise rugs are not as thick and have a denser weave but are nevertheless very useful for keeping the chill off a clipped horse's back.

Thermatex driving
exercise rug on a
harnessed horse

wool exercise rug

Waterproof Exercise Rugs

There are several versions of this type of exercise rug. They are lined with a warm material such as fleece or fake fur or a light blanket and have a waterproof outer and are designed to keep the horse warm and completely dry. Most of these rugs have a breathable outer so that the horse does not sweat up under it even during quite vigorous exercise.

TO FIT The conventional-shape exercise rug should be fitted under the saddle. You place the rug onto the horse's back and put your numnah or saddle square on top, making sure all surfaces are lying smoothly on the horse's back and that there are no wrinkles to cause a rub or a pressure sore. Place you saddle on top and make sure you pull the exercise rug as well as the numnah well up into the gullet of the saddle before you girth the saddle up. There is an exercise rug that has a cut-away area for the saddle. This rug rests on the horse's quarters and is then placed under the saddle flaps and Velcroed closed on the horse's withers just in front of the saddle. This type of exercise rug enables the rider to sit safely on the saddle and have the exercise rug properly secured without

waterproof exercise rug fitted under the saddle

waterproof exercise rug with cut-away area

having to place it under the saddle, which is very useful if your horse has little available room for any extra bulk under the saddle. It also makes things easier if you are just working your horse in and wish to take the exercise rug off when the horse has warmed up.

Reflective Wear

Exercising and hacking out on today's busy roads is always potentially hazardous. The sooner all drivers – either those who are considerate or those who are not so understanding – see you, the safer you and your horse will be, particularly in poor light.

There are several ways that you can be seen without having your horse festooned with too many additional pieces of equipment that may cause an accident if not securely fastened.

Exercise rugs

A reflective exercise rug, either of the conventional or cut-away shape, with a reflective fillet strap will make your horse instantly visible from behind. Make sure you choose a good quality one that is pliable and substantial so that it will not flap or crackle in the wind and possibly spook your horse. It should fit the horse well without hanging over the tail.

Riders tabards or jackets and helmet covers

Reflective clothing for the rider is a good way to be seen by both following and oncoming traffic. Again, make sure these items are well made and will not crackle or flap.

Leg bands and rein and bridle strips

There is a huge range of reflective items to choose from. I think that they are all useful if used sensibly. Try to decide which will make your horse visible without going to extremes and choose well made and securely fastened items that will stay on and stay in place safely.

Brushing Boots

Reflective brushing boots cover a substantial area of your horse's legs and thus make him visible from ground level as well as higher up. As with all leg protection, make sure the boots fit well, do not rub and that they protect the horse's legs as well as make him more visible.

14

Waterproof and Breathable Rugs

Waterproof Rugs

If a rug is waterproof it simply means that the rug stops rain, wind and snow from penetrating the fabric of the rug thus keeping your horse or pony warm and dry. This type of material cannot breath which means that if your horse sweats inside the rug the moisture cannot get away and will lie in between the horse and the rug making the horse's hair wet along the top of the back until the heat of the body dries it out again.

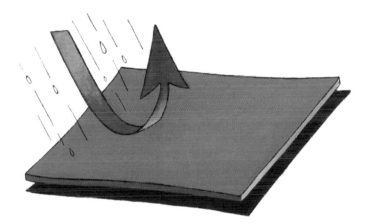

the principles of waterproofing

Waterproof and Breathable Rugs

'Breathable' is the term manufacturers use to describe rugs that allow moisture (the horse's sweat) to pass through the rug's layers and evaporate in the atmosphere. Better quality materials allow this evaporation process to happen quickly but poorer quality materials take longer to complete the process. If your horse has been active and sweated up under his rug, the top of his back can remain wet until the poorer quality material eventually allows the moisture to pass through and evaporate. This might, sometimes, lead you to believe that a waterproof rug is leaking which is not always the case.

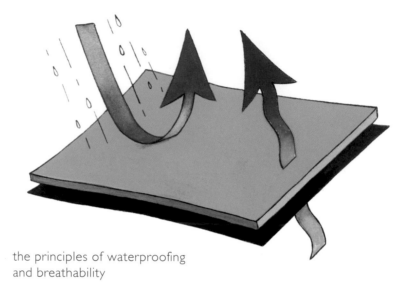

the principles of waterproofing and breathability

15

The Care and Cleaning of Rugs

As with everything, the better you look after something the longer it should last. Rugs should be cleaned every year, preferably in spring when you finish with them, and not left in a heap until October when you suddenly realise you need them again.

You would not believe how much pressure is put on tack shops when they receive rugs for cleaning. There is always a mad rush to get people's rugs cleaned for them at the first sign of bad weather when it is known full well that the rugs have been lying around dirty for probably six months. If your rugs are wet when they come off your horse for the last time, hang them up and dry them out before sending them off to be cleaned and put them into a large plastic sack to transport them to your tack shop or rug cleaner. These few simple actions make the lives of tack shop staff much easier.

If a rug has been damaged and you still need to use it on your horse, try to make sure the rug is as clean and dry as possible for the saddler to deal with. You may have just come from the yard and be dressed for the outdoors and dirt but your saddler is clean and tidy doing business in a dry environment, so show a little consideration. They may be able to repair simple things while you wait if the rug is in a good enough state to handle but if the rug is filthy and smelly, and I speak from experience, it is completely unrealistic and unfair to expect it to be mended without being cleaned first. We have had rugs handed in in a real state with demands being made to have the rug back mended the same day.

Canvas turnout rugs

These rugs need a lot of maintenance. When they are taken to be cleaned they first have to be power-hosed to remove the worst of the dirt, then they are machine washed which cleans them thoroughly but destroys their ability to repel water. They then have to be hung and completely dried; all repairs, if any, are done at this stage. Then the rugs have to be re-proofed, this is a laborious task entailing a re-proofing wax being hand painted all over the rug. Finally they have to be dried again. This whole process, depending on the weather to help with the drying processes, can take up to 20 days!

Modern turnout rugs

These are easier to manage as they do not need to be re-proofed because the back of the top layer of material is proofed to repel water. Good quality turnout rugs, if looked after well, have a good life expectancy and if, after a period of years, they begin to let in a little water because the backing is beginning to deteriorate, then you may be able to extend the life for another winter by having a re-proofing solution washed into them. The cleaning process is as follows: the rugs are power-hosed to get the worst of the dirt off then machine washed (it is very important that the rugs are washed in a mild cleaning solution so as not to damage the material) and then they are thoroughly dried. All repairs needed are done at this stage.

Stable rugs

Stable rugs made of modern materials follow the same cleaning regimes as above, they are hosed and then washed in a machine to get them really clean. All repairs are done when they are completely dry.

Useful Addresses

Aerborn Equestrian Ltd
Pegasus House, 198 Sneiton Dale, Nottingham, NG2 4HJ
Tel: 0115 9505631 Fax: 0115 9483273

Weatherbeeta
7 Riverside, Tramway Estate, Banbury, Oxon, OX16 5RL
Tel: 01295 268123

Thermatex Ltd
27–30 Pentwood Industrial Estate, Station Road, Cardigan, Dyfed, SA43 3AD
Tel: 01239 614648 Fax: 01239 621234

Woof Wear
Callywith Gate Industrial Estate, Bodmin, Cornwall, PL31 2RQ
Tel: 01208 78100 Fax: 01208 72349

Tally Ho Farm Saddlery and Polo Shop
Crouch Lane, Winkfield, Nr Windsor, Berkshire, SL4 4RZ
Tel: 01344 885373

Horseware Products Ltd
Quay Street, Dundalk, Co. Louth, Ireland.
Tel: 00 353 42 9489000

The National Sweet Itch Helpline
(Boet Sweet Itch Blanket and Face Hood)
Rhos Uchaf Hall, Llanfynydd, Nr. Wrexham, Flintshire, LL11 5HR
Tel: 01352 771718

Qualtex
Bond Street Works, off Hangingroyd Lane, Hebden Bridge, W. Yorkshire, HX7 7DE
Tel: 01422 844347

Cottage Craft
Park View Mills, Wibsey Park Avenue, Wibsey, Bradford, W. Yorkshire, BD6 3QA
Tel: 01274 711011

Aerborn Equestrian Ltd
US distributor: Dover Saddlery

Weatherbeeta
US distributor: Weatherbeeta USA
1 877 927 4337
e-mail: info@weatherbeetausa.com

Thermatex Ltd
US distributors: Horse Country Ltd & Libertyville Saddle Shop

Woof Wear
US distributor: Dover Saddlery

Horseware Products Ltd
US distributor: Horseware North America
(1-800-TURNOUT, www.horseware.com)

US horse suppliers:

Dover Saddlery
PO Box 1100, Littleton, MA 01460
1 800 989 1500
www.doversaddlery.com

Horse Country Ltd
60 Alexandra Pike, Warrenton, VA 20186
1 800 882 4868

Libertyville Saddle Shop
PO Box M, Libertyville, IL 60048
1 800 872 3353
www.saddleshop.com

Miller's
350 Page Road, Washington, NC 27889
1 800 553 7655
www.millerharness.com

State Line Tack
PO Box 935, Brockport, NY 14420
1 800 228 9208
www.statelinetack.com

Index